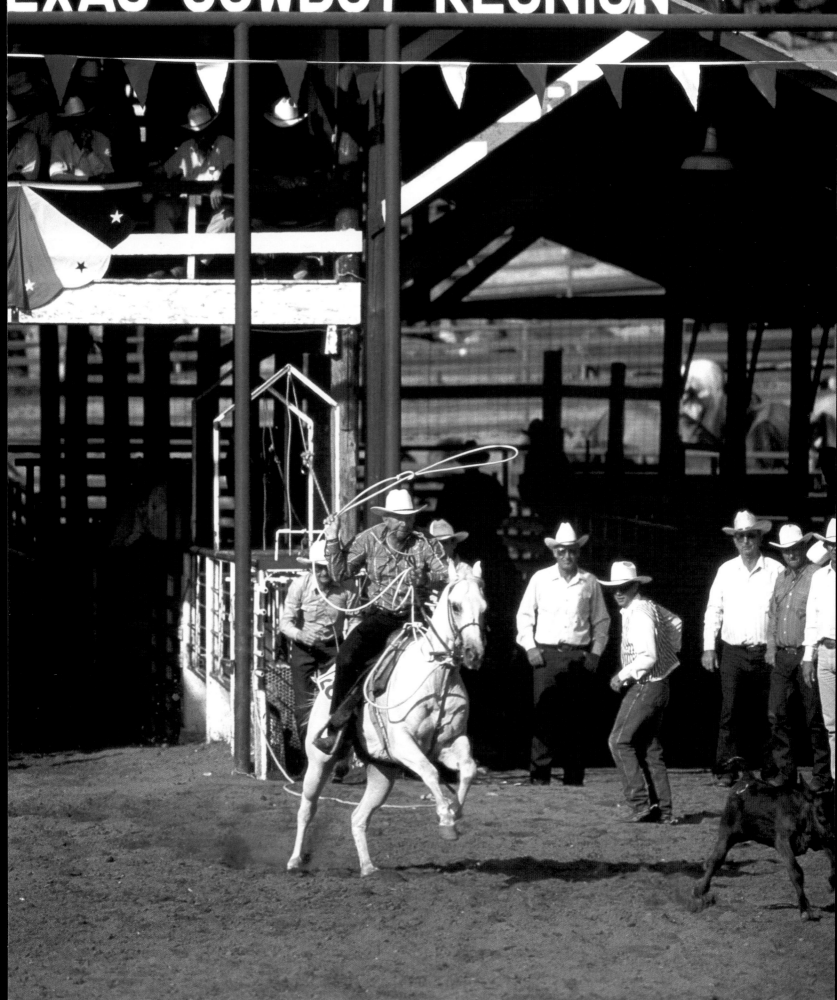

Our
TEXAS

Voyageur Press

Printed in China

05   06   07   08   5   4   3   2

Library of Congress Cataloging-in-Publication Data
Our Texas / edited by Kari Cornell.
    p. cm.
  ISBN 0-89658-637-5 (hardcover)
 1. Texas—Pictorial works. 2. Texas—History, Local—
Pictorial works. I. Cornell, Kari A.
  F387.O94 2004
  976.4'064'0222—dc22
                            2003026526

Distributed in Canada by Raincoast Books,
9050 Shaughnessy Street, Vancouver, B.C. V6P 6E5

Published by Voyageur Press, Inc.
123 North Second Street, P.O. Box 338,
Stillwater, MN 55082 U.S.A.
651-430-2210, fax 651-430-2211
books@voyageurpress.com
www.voyageurpress.com

Educators, fundraisers, premium and gift buyers, publicists, and marketing managers: Looking for creative products and new sales ideas? Voyageur Press books are available at special discounts when purchased in quantities, and special editions can be created to your specifications. For details contact the marketing department at 800-888-9653.

Page 1: *Texas is known for its stunning array of wildflowers. Bluebonnets, which grow along this fence with paintbrush and buttercup, are the state flower. (Photograph © Laurence Parent)*

Page 2: *The first light of day filters through the oak leaves that frame a small waterfall at McKinney Falls State Park near Austin. (Photograph © Richard Reynolds)*

Page 3: *El Capitan Peak in Guadalupe Mountains National Park provides a great view of the surrounding desert grasslands. (Photograph © Laurence Parent)*

Page 4, top: *A pair of cowboy boots from Luchese Boots in San Antonio make a great Texas souvenir. (Photograph © Lee Foster)*

Page 4, bottom: *Autumn grasses catch the brilliant glow of the setting sun in Rita Blanca National Grasslands, located in the northeastern corner of the Texas Panhandle. (Photograph © Richard Reynolds)*

Page 5: *A cowboy sets out to rope a calf at the Texas Cowboy Reunion Rodeo in Stamford. (Photograph © Richard Reynolds)*

Title page: *The Rio Grande River winds through the arid but beautiful land of Big Bend National Park. (Photograph © Zandria Muench Beraldo)*

Title inset: *The great state of Texas graces this weathered wood shutter on a house in Hondo. (Photograph © Carolyn Fox/Image West Photograpy)*

Facing page: *Mission San Francisco de la Espada, completed in 1756, is one of five missions in the San Antonio area. (Photograph © Richard Reynolds)*

Above: *Big Bend's Grapevine Hills are known for their massive granite boulders, a few of which fell together long ago to create the Granite Window. (Photograph © David Muench)*

Left: *Big Bend is home to the nocturnal javelina, an animal that looks like a wild pig but is more closely related to the horse. (Photograph © Michael H. Francis)*

Facing page: *The muddy Rio Grande flows through the towering limestone walls of Santa Elena Canyon in Big Bend National Park. (Photograph © Richard Reynolds)*

Seasonal rains create beautiful waterfalls in the Chisos Mountains, a range formed long ago by volcanic uplift. (Photograph © Laurence Parent)

Bluebonnets blend with prickly pear cacti in Big Bend National Park. (Photograph © Richard Reynolds)

To the west of Big Bend, the adobe walls of an abandoned building in the ghost town of Terlingua appear golden in the evening light. (Photograph © Tom Till)

Facing page: *The century plant, once a source of food for Native Americans, thrives in the arid lands that border the Chisos Mountains. (Photograph © David Muench)*

Above: *Snow storms commonly blanket the Chisos Mountains in a brilliant dusting of white powder during the winter months. (Photograph © Richard Reynolds)*

Benjamin Leaton founded Fort Leaton as a trading post in 1848. The Texas Parks and Wildlife Department now runs the fort as a museum. (Photographs © Laurence Parent)

The U.S. Army established Fort Davis in 1854 to protect those traveling along the nearby San Antonio–El Paso and Chihuahua Trails. (Photograph © Laurence Parent)

The very first rodeo is said to have been held in Pecos, Texas, on July 4, 1883. These days, crowds gather at the Pecos Rodeo Arena each year around the Fourth of July to watch cowboys compete in the West of the Pecos Rodeo. (Photographs © Richard Reynolds)

Facing page: *Limestone cliffs tower above pristine emerald pools as the Pecos River winds its way toward the Amistad International Reservoir near Del Rio, Texas. (Photograph © David Muench)*

Above: *Petroglyphs, etched by people who lived in the caves and rocky shelters along the Lower Pecos River about 6,000 years ago, cover the walls of Painted Canyon. (Photograph © David Muench)*

Near Rocksprings, Texas, on the Edwards Plateau, Devil's Sinkhole plunges almost 400 feet into the earth. The vertical cave provides the perfect home for Brazilian freetail bats and cave swallows. (Photograph © Laurence Parent)

Over the years, the many rivers in the Texas Hill Country have worn away the Tufa limestone to create attractions such as Natural Bridge Caverns (above) and the Caves of Sonora (left). (Photographs © John Elk III)

Above, top: *The lush grasslands and mild climate of the Davis Mountains region attract white-tailed deer and other wildlife. (Photograph © Michael H. Francis)*

Above, bottom: *Autumn is a beautiful time of year in the tranquil Davis Mountains. (Photograph © Laurence Parent)*

Right: *A drive along Texas Highway 166, part of the seventy-four-mile Davis Mountains Scenic Loop, provides breathtaking sunset views. (Photograph © Laurence Parent)*

Mountain bikers test their skills in the Franklin Mountains, one of the best places for the sport in the state. (Photograph © Laurence Parent)

North Franklin Peak, shown here with a rainbow halo, is the focal point of 23,863-acre Franklin Mountains State Park, which lies west of El Paso. (Photograph © Laurence Parent)

Above: *Downtown El Paso still sleeps as the sun rises over the Franklin Mountains. (Photograph © Laurence Parent)*

Right: *Socorro Mission was the second mission established in 1681 along El Camino Real near El Paso. (Photograph © John Elk III)*

Vibrant murals, called Los Murales, decorate walls and shop fronts throughout El Paso. The Chamizal National Memorial marks the U.S.–Mexican border and commemorates the settlement of a land dispute between the two countries. (Photograph © Tom Till)

El Paso's Tigua Cultural Center celebrates the life of the oldest ethnic group in Texas with dance performances, bread-baking demonstrations, and history exhibits. (Photograph © John Elk III)

Rock climbers descend on Hueco Tanks State Historical Park each year between October and April to scale some of the most well-known walls in the sport. (Photograph © Laurence Parent)

Above: *The Hueco Tanks for which the park is named are natural basins in the rock that have trapped rain for thousands of years, providing a reliable water source to animals and people living in the area. (Photograph © David Muench)*

Left: *Hueco Tanks State Park is home to more than 2,000 pictographs, some of which are believed to be 5,000 years old. (Photograph © David Muench)*

Right: *Chili cookoffs, such as this one in Brewster County, are held all over Texas throughout the year. The contests are some of the best places to sample the state's official dish. (Photograph © Richard Reynolds)*

Below: *The longhorn steers that roam the West Texas plains are the state's official large mammal. (Photograph © John Elk III)*

Dust flies as a group of cowboys drive horses through Guadalupe Mountains National Park. (Photograph © Richard Reynolds)

At 8,085 feet, beautiful El Capitan catches the first golden rays of morning sunshine. (Photograph © Tom Till)

Above: *Autumn is perhaps the best time of the year to visit the Guadalupe Mountains, as fall foliage makes for stunning views and daytime temperatures are idyllic. (Photograph © Richard Reynolds)*

Left: *Evidence of the vast ocean that once covered areas of Texas, New Mexico, and Mexico lies here in the reef rocks that remain stacked in the Guadalupe Mountains. (Photograph © David Muench)*

Facing page: *Locals and tourists alike make attempts to polish off the seventy-two-ounce steak dinner at the Big Texan Steak Ranch. Those who are able to finish the entire meal in less than one hour eat for free! (Photograph © Larry Angier/Image West Photography)*

Left: *One downtown Amarillo skyscraper captures the reflections of two other buildings on a sunny Texas day. (Photograph © John Elk III)*

Below: *The Amarillo Livestock Auction, believed to be one of the world's largest, takes place every Tuesday morning. (Photograph © John Elk III)*

Although Route 66 is no longer the main thoroughfare through Amarillo, nostalgia buffs still make regular pilgrimages to see the hotels and restaurants that line this famous stretch of pavement. (Facing page, top and above: photographs © Pedar Ness/Coolstock. Facing page, bottom: photograph © Mike Witzel/Coolstock.

Above, top: *Throughout the Texas Panhandle region, prairie dogs have created a system of burrows and mounds called "towns." (Photograph © Richard Reynolds)*

Above, bottom: *The nine-banded armadillo is synonymous with the state of Texas. (Photograph © Erwin & Peggy Bauer)*

Right: *Lake Meredith, the only lake in the Texas Panhandle, is a popular spot for windsurfing, sailing, and fishing enthusiasts. (Photograph © Laurence Parent)*

Left: *The sun sets on the brilliant red rock walls of Palo Duro Canyon in Palo Duro Canyon State Park. The park, which is filled with towering rock formations such as Lighthouse Rock shown here, is known as "The Grand Canyon of Texas." (Photograph © Laurence Parent)*

Above: *Cottonwood leaves scatter across the red rocks of the canyon in autumn. (Photograph © Laurence Parent)*

*Windmills and old barns, remnants of the pre–Dust Bowl
farmsteads, still stand in the stark but beautiful Rita Blanca
Grasslands in the far northwestern corner of the Panhandle.
(Photograph © Richard Reynolds)*

A good irrigation system is key to growing crops like milo in the Texas Panhandle, an area often plagued by drought. (Photograph © Carolyn Fox/Image West Photography)

Facing page: *At forty-seven feet tall, Tex Randall is one of the tallest Texans around. The concrete giant has stood his ground near Canyon since 1959. (Photograph © Larry Angier/Image West Photography)*

Above: *An old billboard urging Americans to buy victory bonds and stamps for the war effort still decorates a building in downtown Spearman, Texas. (Photograph © Carolyn Fox/ Image West Photography)*

Left: *The flag of the Lone Star State waves in the breeze on the Texas A&M University campus in Canyon, Texas. (Photograph © Carolyn Fox/Image West Photography)*

The blades of J. B. Buchanan's vintage windmill collection spin in tandem from a park in Spearman, Texas. (Photograph © Carolyn Fox/Image West Photography)

In the early 1900s, the Fort Worth Stockyards (above) were the largest in the world. Today the district is on the National Register of Historic Places, and restaurants, shops, and galleries make it a fun place to spend an afternoon. A giant cowboy boot marks this boot and saddle shop (right and facing page) in the Fort Worth Stockyards National Historic District. (Right: photograph © Laurence Parent. Above and facing page: photographs © John Elk III)

Fort Worth's "Cow Town" past is reflected in its strong ranching heritage. Public art displays in the Stockyards and throughout Fort Worth celebrate the tradition of the cattle drive, including those that took place along the Chisholm Trail between 1867 and 1875 (above and facing page, top). And, cowboys still gather at the Stockyards to buy or auction off livestock once a week (facing page, bottom). (Above: photograph © John Elk III. Facing page photographs © Lee Foster)

1867 CHISHOLM TRAIL 1875

Above: *Authentic Mexican food and drink tastes especially good on a sunny afternoon at an outdoor café in Fort Worth. (Photograph © Richard Reynolds)*

Facing page, top: *In the 1970s, old warehouses and factories in Dallas's West End District were renovated to house restaurants, shops, and galleries. (Photograph © John Elk III)*

Facing page, bottom: *Since the beginning of the twentieth century, farmers have been trucking fresh fruits and vegetables to the Dallas Farmers Market at the intersection of Pearl and Cadiz Streets. Today, it's the largest urban farmers market in the country. (Photograph © John Elk III)*

Above: *Neon lights brighten Dallas Alley, a popular shopping center in the West End District. (Photograph © Mike Witzel/ Coolstock)*

Right: *The Dallas skyline glimmers in the golden light of the setting sun. (Photograph © Laurence Parent)*

Facing page: *Brilliant fall color adds yet another dimension of beauty to the bald cypress trees in Caddo Lake State Park. The waterway, which is part of the East Texas Piney Woods, straddles the Texas-Louisiana border. (Photograph © Richard Reynolds)*

Above: *Pine cones and the leaves of magnolia, sassafras, and oak trees blanket the forest floor in Big Thicket National Preserve. (Photograph © David Muench)*

A small stream flows through private land in Jasper County.
(Photograph © Laurence Parent)

Some believe that Nacagdoches is the oldest town in Texas, first settled when the Spaniards established a mission here in 1716. This rustic cabin is one of twelve buildings that date from between 1820 and 1905 in Millard's Crossing, located north of town. (Photograph © David Muench)

Above: *Miles of trails wind through the towering trees of Big Thicket National Preserve, 300,000 acres of wooded swampland located north of Beaumont. (Photograph © John Elk III)*

Left: *Luminescent pitcher plants are naturally designed to trap the insects that the carnivorous plants need to survive. (Photograph © David Muench)*

Facing page: *Sunlight filters through the trees rooted in Black Creek Slough, part of Big Thicket National Preserve. (Photograph © David Muench)*

Above: *Dawn breaks on downtown Houston, the fourth-largest city in the United States. (Photograph © John Elk III)*

Facing page: *The discovery of oil at Beaumont in 1901 spurred an oil boom unlike any other in American history. (Photograph © David Muench)*

Stately homes with beautiful, manicured gardens characterize neighborhoods like Bayou Bend (facing page) *and the Riveroaks District* (above) *in Houston. (Photographs © John Elk III)*

Above: *The Trube House, built in 1890, even has elaborate marble checkerboard walkways. (Photograph © John Elk III)*

Facing page: *The grand homes found in Galveston's East End District and the beautiful buildings that line The Strand are some of the best examples of Victorian architecture in the country. Bishops Palace, built in 1886, is the grandest of them all with twenty-four rooms. (Photograph © David Muench)*

Facing page: *Each December, the city of Galveston celebrates Dickens on the Strand, a weekend of fine dining, concerts, and theatrical performances in the spirit of Charles Dickens's* A Christmas Carol. *(Photograph © Richard Reynolds)*

Left and below: *Ornate Victorian buildings line The Strand, which takes its name from the famous street in London. A hurricane in 1900 spared these buildings and they've since been restored. (Photographs © John Elk III)*

Above: *Oyster shells scatter the beach in Aransas Wildlife Refuge. (Photograph © David Muench)*

Left: *Bolivar Point Lighthouse, built in 1852, guided ships into Galveston Bay until the Civil War, when Confederates tore it down to use as scrap metal. The light was rebuilt in 1872 and it served until it was deactivated in 1933. (Photograph © Laurence Parent)*

George Fulton built the Fulton Mansion in the style of the French Second Empire in the 1870s. Now part of Fulton Mansion State Historical Structure, the home, which overlooks Aransas Bay, is open for public tours. (Photograph © Laurence Parent)

Left: *Alligators make their home in the coastal marshes of the Aransas Wildlife Refuge. (Photograph © Erwin and Peggy Bauer)*

Facing page and below: *Live oaks thrive among the wildflowers and grasslands of the Aransas Wildlife Refuge on the Gulf Coast. (Photographs © David Muench)*

The beautiful wind-swept dunes of Matagorda Island State Park provide a haven for white-tailed deer, coyotes, American alligators, sea turtles, and abundant waterfowl species. (Photograph © Laurence Parent)

As the sun begins to rise, sailboats anchored in the Corpus Christi marina emerge from a tranquil mist. (Photograph © Laurence Parent)

Above: *Nine historic homes, which date from as far back as 1851, have been preserved in Corpus Christi's Heritage Park. (Photograph © John Elk III)*

Left: *Corpus Christi's greatest asset is its waterfront. More than just a place to walk, sail, or relax, the waterfront is home to a major shipping port, the commercial fishing industry, and the nearby Naval Station of Ingleside. (Photograph © Laurence Parent)*

Above: *Waves roll into Padre Island National Seashore, a 113-mile-long barrier island of white sand beaches that stretches along the Texas Gulf Coast. (Photograph © Richard Reynolds)*

Right: *As the tide recedes from Brazos Island, sea shells once tossed and turned by the waves become embedded in the wet sand. (Photograph © David Muench)*

Padre Island is the place for sun and fun on the Texas Gulf Coast. (Above: photographs © Richard Reynolds. Right: photograph © John Elk III)

Spanish moss clings to tree limbs in Santa Ana Wildlife Refuge, 2,000 acres of protected land along the banks of the lower Rio Grande. The reserve is a haven for birds and other wildlife. An estimated 400 species of birds, including the white ibis, the tricolored heron, and the golden-winged warbler, can be seen in the refuge. (Above: photograph © David Muench. Left: photograph © Richard Reynolds)

Facing page: *The prickly pear cactus grows vigorously in the dry desert conditions of the Rio Grande Plains. (Photograph © Richard Reynolds)*

Above: *Agriculture thrives in Mission, Texas, on the fertile land that borders the lower Rio Grande. Mission is known for its ruby red grapefruit and poinsettias, but more common crops like cabbage are cultivated here too. (Photograph © David Muench)*

Above: *The missions of San Antonio are connected by a twelve-mile trail maintained by the National Park Service. Mission San Francisco de la Espada anchors the southern end of the trail. Completed in 1756, the mission served as a training center for the study of arts such as weaving and blacksmithing. (Photograph © Laurence Parent)*

Facing page: *San Antonio is home to five original Spanish missions, more than any other city in the United States. Mission San Jose, founded in 1720 by Antonio Margil de Jesús and completed in 1782, is the grandest of them all. (Photograph © David Muench)*

Facing page: *The Alamo draws more tourists than any other site in Texas. The Alamo was built in 1724 as a mission, but in the early 1800s, Spanish troops took over the building, expanded it, and began to use it as a fort. (Photograph © Laurence Parent)*

Above: *A statue of Ben Milan, a Texan who led troops in the fight against Mexico, stands near the Alamo. (Photograph © Lee Foster)*

San Antonio is known for its attractive River Walk, a canal loop off the San Antonio River that features a walking path, shopping, and several restaurants with outdoor seating. The River Walk is at its best during the holiday season, when Christmas lights and luminaries add to its already festive atmosphere. (Photograph © Richard Reynolds)

Diners appear to blend in with the eye-catching mural at Mi Terra Restaurant in San Antonio. (Photograph © Lee Foster)

A colorful mural and bronze sculpture adorns the entrance to the Dagenbela Gallery in downtown San Antonio. (Photograph © John Elk III)

The Marketplace, or El Mercado in Spanish (above), is the place to find Mexican leather goods, ceramics, clothing, crafts, and reasonable Mexican food (left) in San Antonio. (Above: photograph © John Elk III. Left: photograph © Lee Foster)

Above and facing pagetop: For nine days in late April, Texans crowd the city streets to celebrate Fiesta San Antonio. Elaborate parades, music, dancing, fairs, food, and rodeos are all part of the fun. (Above: photograph © Richard Reynolds. Facing page, top: photograph © John Elk III)

Left: *A River Walk boat tour is a must for those visiting San Antonio for the first time. (Photograph © Lee Foster)*

In the heart of Texas, between San Antonio and Austin, lie the serene, rolling hills of the Hill Country. German settlers arrived in the area in the mid 1800s, and tourists from Texas and beyond have been visiting ever since. (Photograph © John Elk III)

Above: *Ferdinand Lindheimer, a German immigrant, built this home near New Braunfels on the Comal River in the early 1850s. The home has since been restored and the New Braunfels Conservation Society operates the property as a museum. (Photograph © John Elk III)*

Established in the Texas Hill Country by German immigrants in the 1840s, New Braunfels continues to draw tourists interested in the town's historical sites and outdoor enthusiasts who come to bike through surrounding hills or raft nearby rivers. (Photograph © John Elk III)

Facing page: *The rustic cabin at Old Fischer Store in the Hill Country almost disappears into the surrounding woods. (Photograph © David Muench)*

Above; *A small stream, overflowing with spring run-off, winds its way through a grove of pecan trees. (Photograph © David Muench)*

The very German town of Fredericksburg was founded in 1846, one year after New Braunfels. Some of the older residents still speak German as their first language. (Photograph © John Elk III)

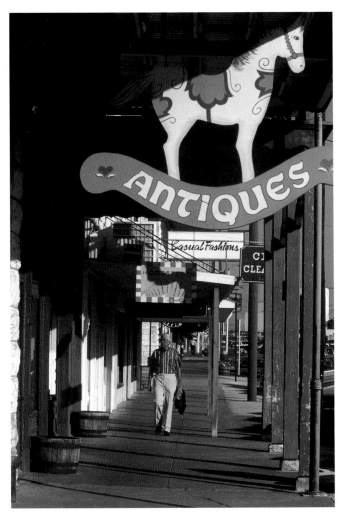

Weekends are busy in Fredericksburg, as people come from nearby San Antonio and Austin to shop for antiques, visit museums, and dine on fine German food. (Left: photograph © John Elk III. Below: photograph © Carolyn Fox/Image West Photography)

Christmas in the Hill Country is a festival of lights. County governments go all out, decorating their courthouses, such as the Blanco County Courthouse shown here (left), with millions of white lights. The Lady Bird Johnson Wildflower Research Center (above) near Austin gets in on the act, too, lighting pretty paper bag luminaries throughout the grounds. (Left: photograph © Richard Reynolds. Above: photograph © Laurence Parent)

Downtown Austin basks in the glow of a brilliant sunset. (Photograph © Laurence Parent)

Above: *The Broken Spoke, one of Austin's many live music clubs, offers classic country and western music in a dance hall setting. (Photograph © Laurence Parent)*

Right: *Mike Slover, saddle and chap craftsman at Austin's Capitol Saddlery, shows off some of his handiwork. (Photograph © Larry Angier/Image West Photography)*

Above: *The Governor's Mansion, built in 1855 in the Greek Revival style, still retains the look and feel of the era. (Photographs © John Elk III)*

Facing page: *The State Capitol Building in Austin, built of red granite in the Renaissance Revival style, is the largest state capitol in the country. (Photograph © Laurence Parent)*

Right: *Austin's Sixth Street Historic District was the town center in the 1870s and 1880s. Since the 1960s, the beautiful Victorian homes and businesses in the neighborhood have been lovingly restored. (Photograph © John Elk III)*

Below: *At 307 feet tall, the University of Texas Tower has a commanding presence on campus. The clock face has a diameter of more than twelve feet. (Photograph © Laurence Parent)*

The stunning gardens within the twenty-two-acre Zilker Botanical Gardens offer a serene, shady respite during Austin's hot summer days. (Photograph © John Elk III)

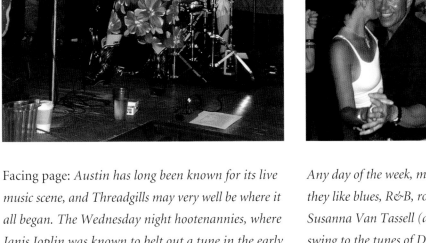

Facing page: *Austin has long been known for its live music scene, and Threadgills may very well be where it all began. The Wednesday night hootenannies, where Janis Joplin was known to belt out a tune in the early 1960s, remain a staple of the restaurant and club today. (Photograph © Mike Witzel/Coolstock)*

Any day of the week, music lovers can catch a show in Austin, whether they like blues, R&B, rock, country, bluegrass, or zydeco. Local favorite Susanna Van Tassell (above, left) plays at Jovita's Cantina while fans swing to the tunes of Dee Lannon & Roger Wallace (above) at the Continental Club, a popular music venue since 1957. (Photographs © Bill Groll, Austin Americana)

Lyndon Baines Johnson lived in this Folk Victorian home, built in Johnson City in 1901, from age five through his high school graduation. It was from this front porch that Johnson announced his candidacy for the U.S. House of Representatives in 1937, the election that launched his political career. (Above: photograph © John Elk III. Right: photograph © Laurence Parent)

Autumn is a beautiful time of year at Lost Maples State Natural Area near Austin, where the high canyon walls that surround the Sabinal River shelter trees and other flora from harsh winds and soaring summertime temperatures. The result is a mini ecosystem where trees not native to the area, such as bigtooth maples, American smoke tree, and witch hazel, thrive. (Photograph © Laurence Parent)

Above: *In the heart of the Texas Hill Country lies Enchanted Rock State Natural Area, home to a giant granite outcropping that rises 425 feet above the ground and extends across 640 acres. (Photograph © Laurence Parent)*

Facing page: *Sunsets over Enchanted Rock accentuate the pink hues inherent in the granite. (Photograph © Richard Reynolds)*

As the sun sets and the heat of the day fades, Enchanted Rock has been known to creak and groan, evidence that the rock is contracting in the cool night air. (Photograph © Laurence Parent)